ALLEN PHOTOG

M000277906

ALL ABOUT
RIDING SIDE-SADDLE

CONTENTS

DIFFERENT TYPES OF SIDE-SADDLE

A CENTURY OF CHANGING STYLE AND FASHION

Side-saddles come in many shapes and sizes, in the same way as the horse and ponies on which they are used.

The majority of side-saddles in use today were made between 1850 and 1939. A small number are still being manufactured, like the new saddle shown here (*see right*).

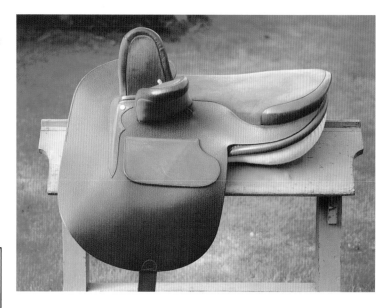

AUTHORS' NOTES

Any schooled horse or pony, from a heavy hunter to a Shetland, should be able to carry a side-saddle.

Doeskin (or suede) affords extra grip for the rider, especially when the seat is doeskin and the pommels are covered in doeskin (*see below*).

Side-saddles are also made with a leather seat and matching leather pommels (*see right*). The leather seat is more hardwearing but does not provide the grip of doeskin or suede.

Occasionally leather-seated side-saddles were made with doeskin-lined pommels: a combination sometimes preferred for hunting and jumping.

A feature on some side-saddles is the adjustable leaping head; the lower pommel can be moved into two or more positions to accommodate different riders and their leg positions.

Another type of side-saddle has the Wykeham pad. The top part of the saddle is retained, and in place of the conventional panel with flocking, there is a detachable thick felt pad. This is less bulky than a flocked panel and therefore can be more suitable for a wide-backed horse or pony.

A more unusual side-saddle is the 'off-side' saddle (*see below*), which enables the rider to sit to the **right** instead of to the **left**.

An alternative to the off-side saddle is a 'reversible pommel' saddle; both pommels can be unscrewed and placed on the near- or off-side, permitting the rider to sit either way (*see photos above*).

Nearly all side-saddles are lined with serge, covered in linen. This facilitates re-flocking as fabric is easier to re-stitch than leather which retains needle holes, weakening the lining over a period of time (*see above*).

Pony saddles, however, sometimes have only a serge lining (without the linen) to give added grip on a rounded pony's back.

Leather-lined side-saddles are not so common, although leather is much harder wearing than fabric. This particular side-saddle (*see above*) is 'flocked' with a single layer of felt to give the widest possible fitting for a cob-type horse or pony.

FITTING THE SIDE-SADDLE

ENSURING A COMFORTABLE FIT FOR HORSE AND RIDER

The size of the side-saddle is very important. If it is **too narrow**, it will pinch and rise up on the withers, tilting the rider back. If it is **too wide** it will move around and be unsafe and uncomfortable for both horse and rider.

The side-saddle must be sufficiently wide to allow a comfortable fit across the withers and down the shoulders, leaving room for the horse's spine.

The underside must be as flat and wide as possible to ensure a wide bearing surface.

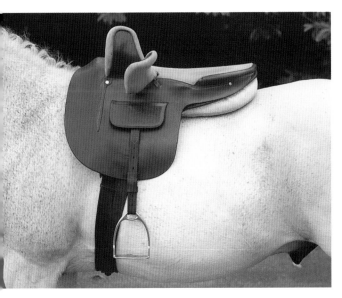

A crupper can help prevent a saddle slipping forward on a rounded pony or cob (*see right*).

The rider must fit the saddle correctly. **Too short** a side-saddle will mean her knee is too far forward and/or her seat is too far back over the edge of the cantle. **Too long** a side-saddle and the rider will be perched on the front and not sitting on the area designed for the seat.

Quick-Release Stirrup Irons and Fittings

Safety Features for the Stirrup Iron or Leather

For the side-saddle rider a quick-release system is essential so that in the event of an emergency her foot does not become ensnared in the stirrup iron and – at the very worst – cause her to be dragged.

There are two ways of dealing with this problem:

1. The stirrup leather and 'quick-release iron'. A conventional stirrup leather, attached to the saddle over a plain metal bar (usually with a leather roller) from which is hung a 'quick-release iron' which opens up in the event of a fall.

Three popular quick-release stirrup irons: **A** and **B** Latchford; **C** Cope; **D** Scott.

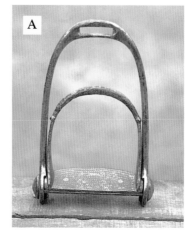

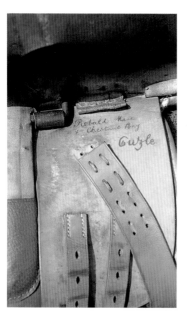

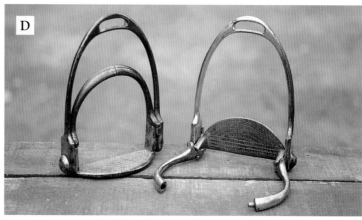

2. The safety stirrup leather
and stirrup iron.
The quick-release
mechanism attached to
the leather allows both
leather and iron to come
away from the saddle
together in the event of
a fall.

Several types of safety
stirrup-leather bar were
patented. The four *main*
side-saddle makers chose
the following three fittings:
Champion & Wilton chose
A for their saddles; both
Mayhew and Whippy chose
B; Owen used **C**.

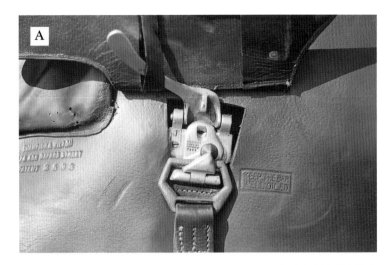

STIRRUP LEATHER ADJUSTMENT

The length of the leather can be adjusted by means of a hook which is attached to the opposite end to the safety fitting: hooked through the appropriate hole, it then has to be covered by the 'keeper', to prevent it rubbing on the rider's boot.

These photos show the fittings on the stirrup leathers plus the adjustment hooks covered by the leather keepers:
D Champion & Wilton; **E** Mayhew and Whippy; **F** Owen.

AUTHORS' NOTE

The Mayhew/Whippy type and the Owen fitting, first produced approximately 100 years ago, are still manufactured today.

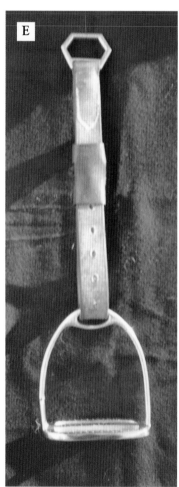

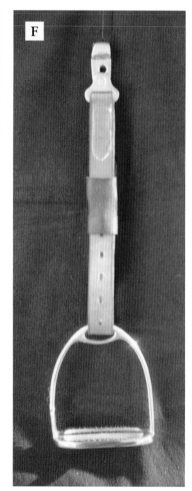

GIRTHING

As with an astride saddle, a side-saddle requires a comfortable girth (preferably a quality three-fold leather for showing, *see right*).

A 'balance' or 'Sefton' girth is generally also used to help keep the saddle in place. It is fitted from the nearside point of the tree, in front of the girth straps, and then diagonally to the rear of the offside of the saddle (*see below*).

It is maintained that the perfectly fitting saddle does not require a balance girth.

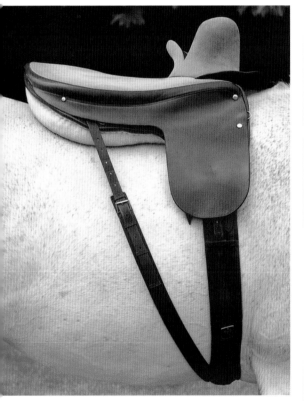

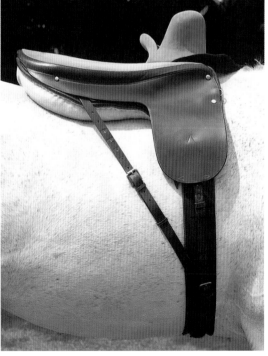

The compromise between the full balance girth and no balance girth is the short balance strap which attaches directly onto the main girth on the offside of the saddle (*see right*).

ADJUSTING THE GIRTH WHEN MOUNTED

Tightening the girths when mounted is only possible from the offside because the rider's legs prevent the flap being lifted on the nearside.

A hook on elastic fixes to an eye on a separate 'overgirth' or 'surcingle' to keep the flap in position when in motion. (The 'overgirth' lies *over* the three-fold and balance girths, and is attached to the tree, under the offside flap. On the nearside it is stitched to the bottom of the saddle flap.)

The alternative method of attachment on the off-side is by using an 'outside' girthing system, i.e. the girth straps lie over the flap.

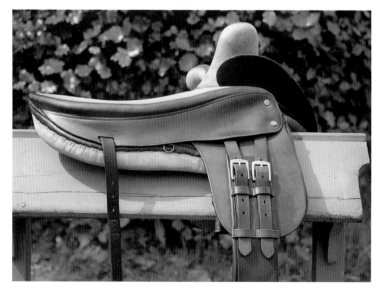

BRIDLE AND REINS

Longer reins are needed when riding side-saddle because the rider sits further back on the horse and standard length reins could become caught up on the fixed pommel or round the knee.

AUTHORS' NOTES

• Double reins (Weymouth or pelham-type bits) should be used when wearing a top hat.

• Bridles should be of plain leather (no coloured browbands for equitation classes).

• Reins may be plain, laced or plaited.

MOUNTING AND DISMOUNTING

MOUNTING WITH A LEG-UP

A competent helper giving a leg-up should put the rider straight into the correct position in the saddle.

The rider's left foot is placed into the helper's cupped hand while the helper is crouched down (*see right*). As the helper lifts the rider, she should help by springing upwards and straightening her left leg (*see below*). Finally, the rider settles into the saddle while the helper still supports her left leg (*see below right*). The helper should be facing forwards throughout the mounting process.

AUTHORS' NOTES

Attempting to mount without assistance or a mounting block is not advisable as it is easy to pull the saddle over and twist the tree.

MOUNTING FROM A MOUNTING BLOCK

A mounting block dispenses with the need for a helper. The easiest way for a novice rider is to mount astride and then adjust her legs.

MOUNTING FROM THE GROUND

Mounting from the ground unaided – if unavoidable – can be mastered only when the rider has had a good deal of practice and can achieve sufficient spring to put her into the saddle. Because the side-saddle stirrup leather is shorter, it is more difficult to reach from the ground; bearing down on the stirrup iron would unbalance the saddle, pulling it over to the nearside. The pommels present a further obstacle, especially when wearing a riding apron.

DISMOUNTING WITH ASSISTANCE

The rider unhooks her legs from the pommels, sits sideways facing the nearside at the back of the saddle, rests her left hand on the upper pommel for support, takes the helper's hand in her left hand and she can then spring lightly to the ground (*see below*).

DISMOUNTING UNAIDED ONTO A MOUNTING BLOCK

The rider stands the horse close to the mounting block, unhooks her legs, as before, moves to the back of the saddle and steps off onto the block.

AUTHORS' NOTES

When dismounting alone, directly onto the ground, the rider must take care to spring far enough away from the saddle to avoid catching herself on the pommels while still holding the reins.

THE CORRECT SEAT

POSITION IN THE SADDLE

In order to maintain the best possible position in the side-saddle the pommels must be correct in shape and size for the rider.

The upper, or 'fixed', pommel supports the rider's right leg. This pommel must be in such a position as to place the right thigh-bone diagonally across the horse, thus distributing the rider's weight evenly from one side to the other. If this pommel is too far to the left for a thin leg, the rider will twist her body round and therefore not remain straight. Should this upper pommel be too curved, the leg will not fit comfortably behind it.

> **AUTHORS' NOTES**
>
> Refer to the *Parts of the Side-saddle* drawing on page 22 showing the position of the pommels (not centre front as an astride saddle).

The lower pommel, also known as the 'leaping head', comes into use when jumping and when an emergency grip is required, giving the rider extra security when needed.

The left leg should hang a hand's breadth under this pommel (*see right*).

> **AUTHORS' NOTES**
>
> The upper, or fixed, pommel cannot be moved or adjusted. It is essential, therefore, that this pommel is in the correct position and of the correct height and curve. (Most side-saddles in use today were bespoke and pommel positions do vary.)

THE HABIT AND TURNOUT

PUTTING ON THE RIDING APRON

The riding apron is made this shape.

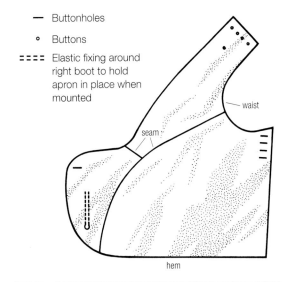

— Buttonholes

° Buttons

==== Elastic fixing around right boot to hold apron in place when mounted

waist

seam

hem

The apron is put on by fastening the buttons on the rider's left hip, with the main body of material being on the rider's right, ready to fit over her right knee when mounted.

To avoid tripping over all this material or dragging it on the ground, the apron is wrapped across the back and secured with one button, when dismounted.

WAISTCOAT AND CUTAWAY JACKET

The close-fitting waistcoat should be either in a contrasting colour, or made to match the habit. It should be seen beneath both jacket lapels and the points should be visible under the cutaway jacket of the modern habit.

Photo **A** shows a modern habit and photo **B** shows a habit cut in the older style.

THE SIDE-SADDLE RIDER'S ACCESSORIES

Tie or silk stock

Tiepin or stockpin

Bun and net

Hairnet

Bowler or top hat

Veil

Leather gloves

Cane

Single spur or spur band

It is correct to wear: a stock with a top hat; 'chamois' gloves with a top hat; brown leather gloves with a bowler; a collar and tie with a bowler; a collar and tie with a bowler and tweed habit.

Veils are worn by ladies (16 and over) and should be secured tightly over the brim of a top hat or bowler.

Canes must be black or brown with a maximum length of 39 in (1 m) for ladies and 30 in (76 cm) for Juniors.

See photos on opposite page

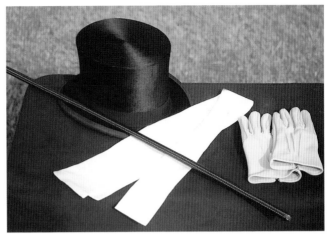

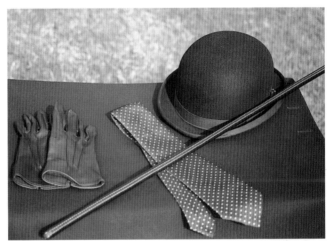

AUTHORS' NOTES

Side-saddle riding had its heyday in this country in the 1920s and '30s. Today, in the revival of this elegant way of riding, we follow the dress code of the period between the two wars.

CORRECT TURNOUT

The correct turnout for different age groups and disciplines on horses and ponies:

- Children (up to the age of 16) *always* wear a collar and tie and protective headwear.

- Ladies' turnout follows the same basic rules as for showing astride.

- **Working Hunter** and **Mountain and Moorland**
  Tweed habit, collar and tie, bowler (jumping section: protective headwear).

- **Ladies Hunter, Riding Horse, Hacks, etc**
  Plain habit, silk stock and top hat **or** plain habit, collar and tie and bowler.

AUTHORS' NOTES

SAFETY is of prime importance: no one is penalised today for wearing safety equipment, i.e. protective headwear and body protectors.

AUTHORS' NOTES

Traditionally, silk top hats should be worn only at Royal Shows and in the afternoon. This rule has, however, become more relaxed recently and top hats are to be seen at all levels.

BASIC GAITS

WALK, TROT AND CANTER

When sitting correctly in the side-saddle, the basic gaits are ridden the same as when riding astride – the only difference being that the right leg is replaced by the cane.

Walk (*above*)

Trot (*right*)

Sitting trot can be more comfortable and less tiring than rising to the trot when seated side-saddle.

Canter (*right*)

The right lead canter is easier to sit into than the left lead. The left lead is shown in this photograph.

A great many horses and ponies accept being ridden side-saddle happily. The rider sitting further back engages the hindquarters, creating impulsion which, in turn, promotes a better ride for the equestrienne and her mount.

JUMPING

Correctly carried out, jumping is enjoyable for horse and rider, whether in the show ring, hunting, or competing cross-country.

The forward position is taught today, i.e. the rider folds forward and shifts the weight to just behind the right knee. The familiar 'backward seat' seen in old prints and pictures is not favoured today.

THE REAR VIEW

Viewed from the rear, it should not be immediately obvious that the rider is sitting side-saddle.

'Seen from behind she appears in the centre of the saddle, the shoulders level with one another, also the hips, and the spine exactly over the spine of her horse; in fact as straight as she would be in a cross-saddle.'

Cross-saddle & Side-saddle
E.V.A. Christy, Seeley,
Service & Co. Ltd,
London, 1932.

PARTS OF THE SIDE-SADDLE

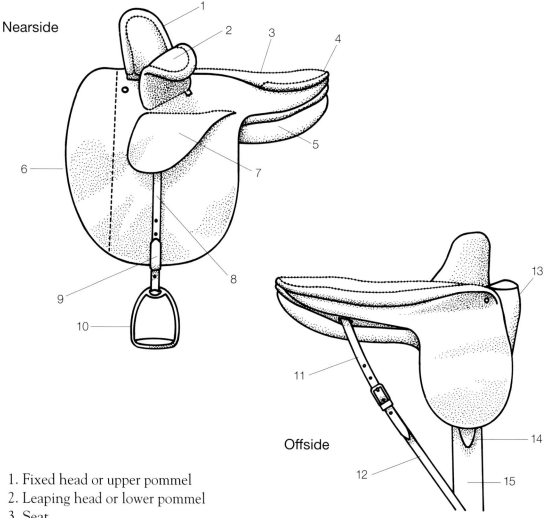

Nearside

Offside

1. Fixed head or upper pommel
2. Leaping head or lower pommel
3. Seat
4. Cantle
5. Panel
6. Saddle flap (including *safe* – forward part of flap shown by dotted line)
7. Skirt covering stirrup bar
8. Stirrup leather
9. Keeper covering hook for adjusting length of leather
10. Stirrup iron
11. Balance girth attachment
12. Balance or Sefton girth
13. Underside of *safe* viewed from offside
14. Leather tab with hook to secure offside flap
15. Girth

For information on joining the

SIDE SADDLE ASSOCIATION

contact:

Mrs R N James
Highbury House
19 High Street
Welford
Northampton NN6 6HT

TEL 01858 575300   FAX 01858 575051

The Side Saddle Association

ACKNOWLEDGEMENTS

Our thanks to Shelley Mitchell, BHSAI, SSA 'B' whose expertise and input, together with that of her horse, Chequers Blue Max, has been invaluable in the production of this book. Shelley is a side-saddle instructor with an excellent reputation; she has a knack for bringing out the best in her pupils and their mounts. Shelley has competed in the Young Riders' Dressage Championships at Goodwood, achieved Supreme Ridden Champion (Side Saddle) at the Annual Beales Show (Bournemouth), and been placed second in the Intermediate Equitation at the National Side Saddle Championships.

British Library Cataloguing-in-Publication Data.
A catalogue record for this book is available from the
British Library

ISBN 0.85131.743.X

© J. A. Allen & Co. Ltd. 1999

Published in Great Britain in 1999 by
J. A. Allen & Company Limited,
1 Lower Grosvenor Place, Buckingham Palace Road,
London, SW1W OEL

Design and Typesetting by Paul Saunders
Series editor Jane Lake
Colour Separation by Tenon & Polert Colour Scanning Ltd.
Printed in Hong Kong by Dah Hua Printing Press Co. Ltd.